D1022022

First published in Great Britain by Brockhampton Press,
a member of the Hodder Headline Group,
20 Bloomsbury Street, London WC1B 3QA

ISBN 1 86019 281 5

Created and produced by Flame Tree Publishing,
part of The Foundry Creative Media Company Limited,
The Long House, Antrobus Road, Chiswick, London W4 5HY

Special thanks to
Kate Brown and Kelley Doak for their work on this series

Printed and bound in U.A.E.

# Wordsworth
## The Eternal Romantic

Written and Compiled by
### K. E. SULLIVAN

# Contents

# *Introduction*

High is our calling, friend! — creative art
(Whether the instrument of words she use,
Or pencil pregnant with ethereal hues,)
Demands the service of a mind and heart ...
(To B. R. Haydon)

WILLIAM WORDSWORTH poured out a tangle of emotion in his poetry; he was passionate about everything, and imbued all he wrote with the same fervour and sense of wonder. The result was poetry that was occasionally repetitive and sometimes dull, a pedantic chronicle of anything and everything because he was unable to discern between the poetic and the mundane and he believed earnestly in all he had to say. Over the years, critics and readers have floundered in the mass of mediocre work which was the result of Wordsworth's laborious efforts. Yet among the plethora of indifferent poetry lay gems which shine more brilliantly than the very best work of his colleagues. For William Wordsworth was a supremely imaginative and graceful poet, producing enduring and unique works which sparkle with vigour, enthusiasm and unparalleled vision.

His passion characterized a tumultuous childhood, and his mother despaired of her emotional and creative son. Wordsworth was born in 1770, at Cockermouth in the heart of the Lake District in England, one of five children in an unremarkable household. His mother died when he was just eight years old and his father, a local solicitor, was so rent by sorrow that he was unable to deal with his eldest boys. He sent William and his brother Richard to school at Hawkhead, where, surrounded by glorious nature, William spent many carefree years, largely unsupervised and free from the strains

of a motherless home. He read eagerly, devouring Fielding and Swift, taking up rowing and skating and spending many long hours walking. The seeds of the poetry of nature were sown, and many years later he recollected them, and allowed them to grow.

When Wordsworth's father died, five years later, the family faced ruin. But his guardians struggled on, and allowed him to stay at Hawkhead, sending him eventually to Cambridge, against all odds. Wordsworth embraced with excitement the social life of his new friends, but despaired of what he considered to be uninspired and boring lectures. He had a disappointing school record and longed mainly for his holidays in the Lake District with his sister Dorothy, whose extraordinary perception both inspired and comforted him. He said of her, 'She gave me eyes, she gave me ears' and her ambition was, in return, to devote her life to him, to his care.

Two years before completing his degree, Wordsworth visited France, ironically on the twilight of the Revolution. As always a passionate idealist, he threw himself into the cause, pledging his support to the revolutionists upon his return to Cambridge. Following the completion of his education, several years later, he returned to France, and met a young girl named Annette Vallon who would eventually give birth to his daughter. He had already returned to England when that news reached him, and war prevented him seeing his daughter or his lover for nearly ten years. He turned in despair to his sister Dorothy, powerless against the machinations of war, personally assaulted by the emotions which waged battle at the centre of his being, and intellectually battered by the collapse of his political ideals. He struggled for some time against depression and went, in 1795, to live with Dorothy. She was able to bring him some comfort, instilling a renewed sense of purpose in her idealistic but serious brother.

Wordsworth's friend, Raisley Calvert, had recently died

and left him £900, enough to hire 'Racedown', a house near Dorset. Here he began a friendship with Coleridge which spawned a close but turbulent relationship. It was through Coleridge that he realized his vocation as a poet and together they planned *Lyrical Ballads* in which *The Rime of the Ancient Mariner* and *Tintern Abbey* appeared. The years in Dorset were marked by a prolific output by both men, and Wordsworth in particular was endlessly excited by the scope of his new career. He and Dorothy travelled to Germany, where the 'Lucy' Poems were written, and then in 1799 they settled at Dove Cottage in Grasmere, the beginning of a quiet existence which provided immeasurable inspiration. They walked together, exchanged ideas and ideals, fed on each other's insights and observations, and became soulmates, each inextricably bound in the other's life. Dorothy was demented by grief, when, in 1802, Wordsworth married her best friend, Mary Hutchinson.

But for Wordsworth these years marked some of his very best work, distinguished by simple rustic tales of country life, emotion, and nature. The pretensions which had marred his earlier work gave way to an uncomplicated understanding of himself and his poetry, and his verse became effortless and perceptive in its sincerity and simplicity. Coleridge had, by this time, followed them to the Lake District. He became deeply unhappy and addicted to drugs, and a great worry to the Wordsworths, who provided moral support for a man who grew increasingly immoral, and nursing care for a man who sought to destroy himself.

When John, his favourite brother, died in 1805, Wordsworth began *The Prelude*, with the intention of presenting it as a gift to Coleridge. He addressed the issues of mortality and found a kind of serenity in his discoveries. At peace with himself, he wrote some of his most eloquent sonnets and verses, and in the form of *The Prelude* one of the most insightful and revealing works ever produced by a poet.

The Wordsworth family expanded to include three children, and Thomas, a fourth was born in 1806. They moved from Dove Cottage, to a larger home in Allan Bank, where a fifth child, Catherine was born. The family was joined there by Coleridge and de Quincy. Wordsworth managed, in this disordered household, to publish works which usually met with disinterest or disdain. He and Coleridge published a magazine entitled *The Friend*, which had a short life, and caused the final breach between the two poets. And then, in 1812, when William and Mary's sixth child was but two, Catherine died, followed by Thomas. They moved to Rydal, and by taking on the office of Distributor of Stamps for Westmoreland, Wordsworth was able to support his family, dedicatedly working on *The Excursion* which was another eighteen years to publication.

From 1816 Wordsworth became increasingly unhappy and his work less and less remarkable. He longed for the fresh innocence of his early years, where his innate belief in the beauty of all that surrounded him provided him with unending inspiration and hope. But financial worries, the deaths of his children, the destruction of his friend Coleridge, all served to suffocate his vision. He turned half-heartedly to the church and wrote his *Ecclesiastical Sonnets*. But they lacked the verve and originality of his earlier work, and the lack of sincerity in his poetry betrayed his growing faithlessness.

But Wordsworth did, at the end of his life, achieve a sudden and overwhelming fame which lead, in 1843, to the post of Poet Laureate. When his favourite daughter Dora died in 1847, his grief threatened to cause his own death, so deep were the wounds of his anguish. He little enjoyed the last decade of his life, and cared for nothing after the death of Dora. *The Recluse*, his last great work, was never finished, but the despair of its author is almost tangible. He struggled with his work in the last years, producing some passages which echoed his earlier brilliance, but more often tedious verse which spoke of nothing at all but Wordsworth's own attempts at poetic grandeur. He died in 1850, one of the greatest poets of the Romantic movement.

## Author's Note

Wordsworth's poetry encompassed various themes throughout his long career. He was as passionate about the daffodils on the hill behind his cottage as he was the cause of the French Revolutionaries, and the subjects of his poetry changed shape with every new enthusiasm. He was prolific and indiscriminate; his work was splendid, and then it was indifferent. The following is a selection of some of his short poems, along with extracts from longer ones. The overwhelming quality that characterizes each is its unique magic, its resounding ability to soar.

# *Chronology*

1770    Wordsworth born, 7 April.

1779    Wordsworth attends Hawkshead Grammar School.

1787    Wordsworth's first published poem 'Sonnet, on Seeing Miss Helen Maria William Weep at a Tale of Distress' appears in *The European Magazine*.

1790    Walking tour of France and Switzerland.

1791    Returns to France, meets Annette Vallon.

1792    Wordsworth's illegitimate daughter Caroline born.

1795    Inherits £900 and goes to live with Dorothy in Dorset.

1797    Completes play, *The Borderers*. Begins great friendship with Coleridge.

1798    Coleridge and Wordsworth publish *Lyrical Ballads*. *The Prelude* begun.

1799    Moves to Dove Cottage in Grasmere.

1802    Marries Mary Hutchinson.

1805    *The Prelude* completed.

1807    *Poems in Two Volumes* published.

1808    Moves to Allan Bank.

1811    Deaths of children, Thomas and Catherine.

1812    Move from Allan Bank to the Rectory, Grasmere.

1813    Becomes distributor of Stamps for Westmoreland. Completes *The Excursion*.

1814    *The Excursion* published. *The Recluse* planned.

1815    First Collected Edition of Poems published.

1820    Publishes *The River Duddon* sequence.

1827    Tours with Rhine with daughter Dora, and Coleridge.

1834    Coleridge dies

1843    Becomes Poet Laureate.

1847    Dora's death.

1850    Wordsworth dies, 23 April. *The Prelude* published by wife and executors.

# An Evening Walk

### ADDRESSED TO A YOUNG LADY
—————— EXTRACT ——————

FAR FROM my dearest Friend, 'tis mine to rove
Through bare grey dell, high wood, and pastoral cove;
Where Derwent rests, and listens to the roar
That stuns the tremulous cliffs of high Lodore;
Where peace to Grasmere's lonely island leads,
To willowy hedge-rows, and to emerald meads;
Leads to her bridge, rude church, and cottaged grounds,
Her rocky sheepwalks, and her woodland bounds;
Where, undisturbed by winds, Winander sleeps;
'Mid clustering isles, and holly-sprinkled steeps;
Where twilight glens endear my Esthwaite's shore,
And memory of departed pleasures, more.

Fair scenes, erewhile, I taught, a happy child,
The echoes of your rocks my carols wild:
The spirit sought not then, in cherished sadness,
A cloudy substitute for failing gladness.
In youth's keen eye the livelong day was bright,
The sun at morning, and the stars at night,
Alike, when first the bittern's hollow bill
Was heard, or woodcocks roamed the moonlight hill.

# The Mother's Return

## BY THE SAME
### —— EXTRACT ——

A MONTH, sweet Little-ones, is past
Since your dear Mother went away, —
And she to-morrow will return;
To-morrow is the happy day.

O blessed tidings! thought of joy!
The eldest heard with steady glee;
Silent he stood; then laughed amain, —
And shouted, 'Mother, come to me!'

Louder and louder did he shout,
With witless hope to bring her near! —
'Nay, patience! patience, little boy;
Your tender mother cannot hear.'

I told of hills, and far-off towns,
And long, long vales to travel through;
He listens, puzzled, sore perplexed,
But he submits; what can he do?

No strife disturbs his sister's breast;
She wars not with the mystery
Of time and distance, night and day;
The bonds of our humanity.

Her joy is like an instinct, joy
Of kitten, bird, or summer fly;
She dances, runs without an aim,
She chatters in her ecstasy.

Her brother now takes up the note,
And echoes back his sister's glee;
They hug the infant in my arms,
As if to force his sympathy.

## A Farewell
—— EXTRACT ——

FAREWELL, thou little Nook of mountain-ground,
Thou rocky corner in the lowest stair
Of that magnificent temple which doth bound
One side of our whole vale with grandeur rare;
Sweet garden-orchard, eminently fair,
The loveliest spot that man hath ever found,
Farewell! – we leave thee to Heaven's peaceful care,
Thee, and the Cottage which thou dost surround.

Our boat is safely anchored by the shore,
And there will safely ride when we are gone;
The flowering shrubs that deck our humble door
Will prosper, though untended and alone;
Fields, goods, and far-off chattels we have none:
These narrow bounds contain our private store
Of things earth makes, and sun doth shine upon;
Here are they in our sight – we have no more.

# To a Butterfly

STAY NEAR me – do not take thy flight!
A little longer stay in sight!
Much converse do I find in thee,
Historian of my infancy!
Float near me; do not yet depart!
Dead times revive in thee:
Thou bring'st, gay creature as thou art!
A solemn image to my heart,
My father's family!

Oh! pleasant, pleasant were the days,
The time, when in our childish plays,
My sister Emmeline and I
Together chased the butterfly!
A very hunter did I rush
Upon the prey; – with leaps and springs
I followed on from brake to bush;
But she, God love her! feared to brush
The dust from off its wings.

# Lucy Gray
## OR SOLITUDE

OFT I HAD heard of Lucy Gray:
And, when I crossed the wild,
I chanced to see at break of day
The solitary child.

No mate, no comrade Lucy knew;
She dwelt on a wide moor,
– The sweetest thing that ever grew
Beside a human door!

You yet may spy the fawn at play,
The hare upon the green;
But the sweet face of Lucy Gray
Will never more be seen.

'To-night will be a stormy night –
You to the town must go;
And take a lantern, Child, to light
Your mother through the snow.'

'That, Father! will I gladly do:
'Tis scarcely afternoon –
The minster-clock has just struck two,
And yonder is the moon!'

At this the Father raised his hook,
And snapped a faggot-band;
He plied his work; – and Lucy took
The lantern in her hand.

Not blither is the mountain roe:
With many a wanton stroke
Her feet disperse the powdery snow,
That rises up like smoke.

The storm came on before its time:
She wandered up and down;
And many a hill did Lucy climb:
But never reached the town.

The wretched parents all that night
Went shouting far and wide;
But there was neither sound nor sight
To serve them for a guide.

At day-break on a hill they stood
That overlooked the moor;
And thence they saw the bridge of wood,
A furlong from their door.

They wept – and, turning homeward, cried,
'In heaven we all shall meet;'
– When in the snow the mother spied
The print of Lucy's feet.

Then downwards from the steep hill's edge
They tracked the footmarks small;
And through the broken hawthorn hedge,
And by the long stone-wall;

And then an open field they crossed:
The marks were still the same;
And tracked them on, nor ever lost;
And to the bridge they came.

They followed from the snowy bank
Those footmarks, one by one,
Into the middle of the plank;
And further there were none!

—Yet some maintain that to this day
She is a living child;
That you may see sweet Lucy Gray
Upon the lonesome wild.

O'er rough and smooth she trips along,
And never looks behind;
And sings a solitary song
That whistles in the wind.

## The Idiot Boy
—— EXTRACT ——

'TIS EIGHT o'clock, – a clear March night,
The moon is up, – the sky is blue,
The owlet, in the moonlight air,
Shouts from nobody knows where;
He lengthens out his lonely shout,
Halloo! halloo! a long halloo!

—Why bustle thus about your door,
What means this bustle, Betty Foy?
Why are you in this mighty fret?
And why on horseback have you set
Him whom you love, your Idiot Boy?

# The Pet-Lamb

*A PASTORAL*
—— EXTRACT ——

THE DEW was falling fast, the stars began to blink;
I heard a voice; it said, 'Drink, pretty creature, drink!'
And, looking o'er the hedge, before me I espied
A snow-white mountain-lamb with a Maiden at its side.

Nor sheep nor kine were near; the lamb was all alone,
And by a slender cord was tethered to a stone;
With one knee on the grass did the little Maiden kneel,
While to that mountain-lamb she gave its evening meal.

The lamb, while from her hand he thus his supper took,
Seemed to feast with head and ears; and his tail
with pleasure shook.
'Drink, pretty creature, drink,' she said in such a tone
That I almost received her heart into my own.

'Twas little Barbara Lewthwaite, a child of beauty rare!
I watched them with delight, they were such a lovely pair.
Now with her empty can the Maiden turned away:
But ere ten yards was gone her footsteps did she stay.

Right towards the lamb she looked; and from a shady place
I unobserved could see the workings of her face:
If Nature to her tongue could measured numbers bring,
Thus, thought I, to her lamb that little Maid might sing:

'What ails thee, young One? what? Why pull so at the cord?
Is it not well with thee? well both for bed and board?
The plot of grass is soft, and green as grass can be;
Rest, little young One, rest; what is't that aileth thee?

# The Childless Father

'UP, TIMOTHY, up with your staff and away!
Not a soul in the village this morning will stay;
The hare has just started from Hamilton's grounds,
And Skiddaw is glad with the cry of the hounds.'

– Of coats and of jackets grey, scarlet, and green,
On the slopes of the pastures all colours were seen;
With their comely blue aprons, and caps white as snow,
The girls on the hills made a holiday show.

Fresh sprigs of green box-wood, not six months before,
Filled the funeral basin at Timothy's door;
A coffin through Timothy's threshold had past;
One Child did it bear, and that Child was his last.

Now fast up the dell came the noise and the fray,
The horse, and the horn, and the hark! hark away!
Old Timothy took up his staff, and he shut
With a leisurely motion the door of his hut.

Perhaps to himself at that moment he said;
'The key I must take, for my Ellen is dead.'
But of this in my ears not a word did he speak;
And he went to the chase with a tear on his cheek.

# Maternal Grief
## —— EXTRACT ——

DEPARTED Child! I could forget thee once
Though at my bosom nursed; this woeful gain
They dissolution brings, that in my soul
Is present and perpetually abides
A shadow, never, never to be displaced
By the returning substance, seen or touched,
Seen by mine eyes, or clasped in my embrace.
Absence and death how differ they! and how
Shall I admit that nothing can restore
What one short sigh so easily removed? –
Death, life, and sleep, reality and thought,
Assist me, God, their boundaries to know,
O teach me calm submission to thy Will!

# Michael

*A PASTORAL POEM*
—— EXTRACT ——

UPON THE forest-side in Grasmere Vale
There dwelt a Shepherd, Michael was his name;
An old man, stout of heart, and strong of limb.
His bodily frame has been from youth to age
Of an unusual strength: his mind was keen,
Intense, and frugal, apt for all affairs,
And in his shepherd's calling he was prompt
And watchful more than ordinary men.
Hence had he learned the meaning of all winds,
Of blasts of every tone; and oftentimes,
When others heeded not, he heard the South
Make subterraneous music, like the noise
Of bagpipers on distant Highland hills.
The Shepherd, at such warning, of his flock
Bethought him, and he to himself would say,
'The winds are now devising work for me!'
And, truly, at all times, the storm, that drives
The traveller to a shelter, summoned him
Up to the mountains: he had been alone
Amid the heart of many thousand mists,
That came to him, and left him, on the heights.
So lived he till his eightieth year was past.

# O Nightingale! Thou Surely Art

O NIGHTINGALE! thou surely art
A creature of a 'fiery heart': —
These notes of thine — they pierce and pierce;
Tumultuous harmony and fierce!
Thou sing'st as if the God of wine
Had helped thee to a Valentine;
A song in mockery and despite
Of shades, and dews, and silent night;
And steady bliss, and all the loves
Now sleeping in these peaceful groves.
I heard a Stock-dove sing or say
His homely tale, this very day;
His voice was buried among trees,
Yet to be come-at by the breeze:
He did not cease; but cooed — and cooed:
And somewhat pensively he wooed:
He sang of love, with quiet blending,
Slow to begin, and never ending;
Of serious faith, and inward glee;
That was the song — the song for me!

# There Was a Boy

THERE WAS a Boy; ye knew him well, ye cliffs
And islands of Winander! – many a time,
At evening, when the earliest stars began
To move along the edges of the hills,
Rising or setting, would he stand alone,
Beneath the trees, or by the glimmering lake;
And there, with fingers interwoven, both hands
Pressed closely palm to palm and to his mouth
Uplifted, he, as through an instrument,
Blew mimic hootings to the silent owls,
That they might answer him. – And they would shout
Across the watery vale, and shout again
Responsive to his call, – with quivering peals,
And long halloos, and screams, and echoes loud
Redoubled and redoubled; concourse wild
Of jocund din! And, when there came a pause
Of silence such as baffled his best skill:
Then sometimes, in that silence, while he hung
Listening, a gentle shock of mild surprise
Has carried far into his heart the voice
Of mountain-torrents; or the visible scene
Would enter unawares into his mind
With all its solemn imagery, its rocks,
Its woods, and that uncertain heaven received
Into the bosom of the steady lake.

This boy was taken from his mates, and died
In childhood, ere he was full twelve years old.
Pre-eminent in beauty is the vale
Where he was born and bred: the church yard hangs
Upon a slope above the village-school;
And through that churchyard when my way has led
On summer-evenings, I believe that there
A long half-hour together I have stood
Mute — looking at the grave in which he lies!


# A Slumber Did My Spirit Seal


A SLUMBER did my spirit seal;
I had no human fears:
She seemed a thing that could not feel
The touch of earthly years.

No motion has she now, no force;
She neither hears nor sees;
Rolled round in earth's diurnal course,
With rocks, and stones, and trees.

# Nutting

IT SEEMS a day
(I speak of one from many singled out)
One of those heavenly days that cannot die;
When, in the eagerness of boyish hope,
I left our cottage-threshold, sallying forth
With a huge wallet o'er my shoulders slung,
A nutting-crook in hand; and turned my steps
Tow'rd some far-distant wood, a Figure quaint,
Tricked out in proud disguise of cast-off weeds
Which for that service had been husbanded,
By exhortation of my frugal Dame –
Motley accoutrement, of power to smile
At thorns, and brakes, and brambles, – and in truth
More ragged than need was! O'er pathless rocks,
Through beds of matted fern, and tangled thickets,
Forcing my way, I came to one dear nook
Unvisited, where not a broken bough
Drooped with its withered leaves, ungracious sign
Of devastation; but the hazels rose
Tall and erect, with tempting clusters hung,
A virgin scene! – A little while I stood,
Breathing with such suppression of the heart

As joy delights in; and with wise restraint
Voluptuous, fearless of a rival, eyed
The banquet; – or beneath the trees I sate
Among the flowers, and with the flowers I played;
A temper known to those who, after long
And weary expectation, have been blest
With sudden happiness beyond all hope.
Perhaps it was a bower beneath whose leaves
The violets of five seasons re-appear
And fade, unseen by any human eye;
Where fairy water-breaks do murmur on
For ever; and I saw the sparkling foam,
And – with my cheek on one of those green stones
That, fleeced with moss, under the shady trees,
Lay round me, scattered like a flock of sheep –
I heard the murmur and the murmuring sound,
In that sweet mood when pleasure loves to pay
Tribute to ease; and, of its joy secure,
The heart luxuriates with indifferent things,
Wasting its kindliness on stocks and stones,
And on the vacant air. Then up I rose,
And dragged to earth both branch and bough, with crash
And merciless ravage: and the shady nook
Of hazels, and the green and mossy bower,
Deformed and sullied, patiently gave up
Their quiet being: and unless I now
Confound my present feelings with the past,
Ere from the mutilated bower I turned
Exulting, rich beyond the wealth of kings,
I felt a sense of pain when I beheld
The silent trees, and saw the intruding sky. –
Then, dearest Maiden, move along these shades
In gentleness of heart; with gentle hand
Touch – for there is a spirit in the woods.

# At Furness Abbey

HERE, WHERE, of havoc tired and rash undoing,
Man left this Structure to become Time's prey,
A soothing spirit follows in the way
That Nature takes, her counter-work pursuing.
See how her ivy clasps the sacred Ruin,
Fall to prevent or beautify decay;
And, on the mouldered walls, how bright, how gay,
The flowers in pearly dews their bloom renewing!
Thanks to the place, blessings upon the hour;
Even as I speak the rising Sun's first smile
Gleams on the grass-crowned top of yon tall Tower,
Whose cawing occupants with joy proclaim
Prescriptive title to the shattered pile,
Where, Cavendish, *thine* seems nothing but a name!

# I Wandered Lonely as a Cloud

I WANDERED lonely as a cloud
That floats on high o'er vales and hills,
When all at once I saw a crowd,
A host of golden daffodils;
Beside the lake, beneath the trees,
Fluttering and dancing in the breeze.

Continuous as the stars that shine
And twinkle on the milky way.
They stretched in never-ending line
Along the margin of a bay:
Ten thousand saw I at a glance,
Tossing their heads in sprightly dance.

The waves beside them danced; but they
Out-did the sparkling waves in glee:
A poet could not but be gay,
In such a jocund company:
I gazed—and gazed—but little thought
What wealth the show to me had brought:

For oft, when on my couch I lie
In vacant or in pensive mood,
They flash upon that inward eye
Which is the bliss of solitude;
And then my heart with pleasure fills,
And dances with the daffodils.

# *Persecution*

LAMENT! for Diocletian's fiery sword
Works busy as the lightning; but instinct
With malice ne'er to deadliest weapon linked,
Which God's ethereal storehouses afford:
Against the Followers of the incarnate Lord
It rages; – some are smitten in the field –
Some pierced to the heart through the ineffectual shield
Of sacred home; – with pomp are others gored
And dreadful respite. Thus was Alban tried,
England's first Martyr, whom no threats could shake;
Self-offered victim, for his friend he died,
And for the faith; nor shall his name forsake
That Hill, whose flowery platform seems to rise
By Nature decked for holiest sacrifice.

# Fancy and Tradition

THE LOVERS took within this ancient grove
Their last embrace; beside those crystal springs
The Hermit saw the Angel spread his wings
For instant flight; the Sage in yon alcove
Sate musing; on that hill the Bard would rove,
Not mute, where now the linnet only sings:
Thus everywhere to truth Tradition clings,
Or Fancy localises Powers we love.
Were only History licensed to take note
Of things gone by, her meagre monuments
Would ill suffice for persons and events:
There is an ampler page for man to quote,
A reader book of manifold contents,
Studied alike in palace and in cot.

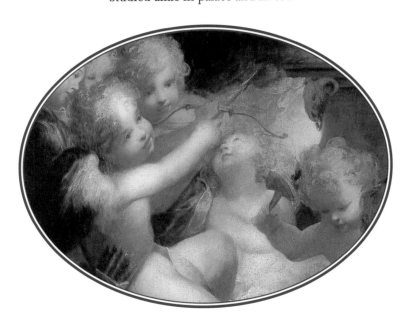

# Expostulation and Reply

'WHY, WILLIAM, on that old grey stone,
  Thus for the length of half a day,
Why, William, sit you thus alone,
  And dream your time away?

'Where are your books? – that light bequeathed
  To Beings else forlorn and blind!
Up! up! and drink the spirit breathed
  From dead men to their kind.

'You look round on your Mother Earth,
  As if she for no purpose bore you;
As if you were her first-born birth,
  And none had lived before you!'

One morning thus, by Esthwaite lake,
  When life was sweet, I knew not why,
To me my good friend Matthew spake,
  And thus I made reply:

'The eye – it cannot choose but see;
  We cannot bid the ear be still;
Our bodies feel, where'er they be,
  Against or with our will.

'Nor less I deem that there are Powers
Which of themselves our minds impress;
That we can feed this mind of ours
  In a wise passiveness.

'Think you, 'mid all this mighty sum
Of things for ever speaking,
That nothing of itself will come,
But we must still be seeking?

'– Then ask not wherefore, here, alone,
Conversing as I may,
I sit upon this old grey stone,
And dream my time away.'

# They Called Thee Merry England

They called Thee MERRY ENGLAND, in old time;
A happy people won for thee that name
With envy heard in many a distant clime;
And, spite of change, for me thou keep'st the same
Endearing title, a responsive chime
To the heart's fond belief; though some there are
Whose sterner judgments deem that word a snare
For inattentive Fancy, like the lime
Which foolish birds are caught with. Can, I ask,
This face of rural beauty be a mask
For discontent, and poverty, and crime;
These spreading towns a cloak for lawless will?
Forbid it, Heaven! – and MERRY ENGLAND still
Shall be thy rightful name, in prose and rhyme!

# The Solitary Reaper

BEHOLD HER, single in the field,
You solitary Highland Lass!
Reaping and singing by herself;
Stop here, or gently pass!
Alone she cuts and binds the grain,
And sings a melancholy strain;
O listen! for the Vale profound
Is overflowing with the sound.

No Nightingale did ever chaunt
More welcome notes to weary bands
Of travellers in some shady haunt,
Among Arabian sands:
A voice so thrilling ne'er was heard
In spring-time from the Cuckoo-bird,
Breaking the silence of the seas
Among the farthest Hebrides.
Will no one tell me what she sings? –

Will no one tell me what she sings? –
Perhaps the plaintive numbers flow
For old, unhappy, far-off things,
And battles long ago:
Or is it some more humble lay,
Familiar matter of to-day?
Some natural sorrow, loss, or pain,
That has been, and may be again?

Whate'er the theme, the Maiden sang
As if her song could have no ending;
I saw her singing at her work,
And o'er the sickle bending; –
I listened, motionless and still;
And, as I mounted up the hill,
The music in my heart I bore,
Long after it was heard no more.

# The Tables Turned
### AN EVENING SCENE ON THE SAME SUBJECT

UP ! UP ! my Friend, and quit your books;
Or surely you'll grow double:
Up ! up ! my Friend, and clear your looks;
Why all this toil and trouble?

The sun, above the mountain's head,
A freshening lustre mellow
Through all the long green fields has spread,
His first sweet evening yellow.

Books! 'tis a dull and endless strife:
Come, hear the woodland linnet,
How sweet his music! on my life,
There's more of wisdom in it.

And hark! how blithe the throstle sings!
He, too, is no mean preacher:
Come forth into the light of things,
Let Nature be your Teacher.

She has a world of ready wealth,
Our minds and hearts to bless –
Spontaneous wisdom breathed by health,
Truth breathed by cheerfulness.

One impulse from a vernal wood
May teach you more of man,
Of moral evil and of good,
Than all the sages can.

Sweet is the lore which Nature brings;
Our meddling intellect
Mis-shapes the beauteous forms of things: –
We murder to dissect.

Enough of Science and of Art;
Close up those barren leaves;
Come forth, and bring with you a heart
That watches and receives.

## Glad Tidings

FOR EVER hallowed be this morning fair,
Blest be the unconscious shore on which ye tread,
And blest the silver Cross, which ye, instead
Of martial banner, in procession bear;
The Cross preceding Him who floats in air,
The pictured Saviour! – By Augustin led,
They come – and onward travel without dread,
Chanting in barbarous ears a tuneful prayer –
Sung for themselves, and those whom they would free!
Rich conquest waits them: – the tempestuous sea
Of Ignorance, that ran so rough and high
And heeded not the voice of clashing swords,
These good men humble by a few bare words,
And calm with fear of God's divinity.

# Lines Written in Early Spring

I HEARD a thousand blended notes,
While in a grove I sate reclined,
In that sweet mood when pleasant thoughts
Bring sad thoughts to the mind.

To her fair works did Nature link
The human soul that through me ran;
And much it grieved my heart to think
What man has made of man.

Through primrose tufts, in that green bower,
The periwinkle trailed its wreaths;

And 'tis my faith that every flower
Enjoys the air it breathes.

The birds around me hopped and played,
Their thoughts I cannot measure: –
But  the least motion which they made,
It seemed a thrill of pleasure.

The budding twigs spread out their fan,
To catch the breezy air;
And I must think, do all I can,
That there was pleasure there.

If this belief from heaven be sent,
If such be Nature's holy plan,
Have I not reason to lament
What man has made of man?

# Ode to Duty

STERN DAUGHTER of the Voice of God!
O Duty! if that name thou love
Who art a light to guide, a rod
To check the erring, and reprove;
Thou, who art victory and law
When empty terrors overawe;
From vain temptations dost set free;
And calm'st the weary strife of frail humanity!

There are who ask not if thine eye
Be on them; who, in love and truth,
Where no misgiving is, rely
Upon the genial sense of youth:
Glad Hearts! without reproach or blot;
Who do thy work, and know it not:
Oh! if through confidence misplaced
They fail, thy saving arms, dread Power! around them cast.

Serene will be our days and bright,
And happy will our nature be,
When love is an unerring light,
And joy its own security.
And they a blissful course may hold
Even now, who, not unwisely bold,
Live in the spirit of this creed;
Yet seek thy firm support, according to their need.

I, loving freedom, and untried;
No sport of every random gust,
Yet being to myself a guide,
Too blindly have reposed my trust:
And oft, when in my heart was heard
Thy timely mandate, I deferred
The task, in smoother walks to stray;
But thee I now would serve more strictly, if I may.

Through no disturbance of my soul,
Or strong compunction in me wrought,
I supplicate for thy control;
But in the quietness of thought:
Me this unchartered freedom tires;
I feel the weight of chance-desires:
My hopes no more must change their name,
I long for a repose that ever is the same.

[Yet not the less would I throughout
Still act according to the voice
Of my own wish; and feel past doubt
That my submissiveness was choice:
Not seeking in the school of pride
For 'precepts over dignified,'
Denial and restraint I prize
No farther than they breed a second Will more wise.]

Stern Lawgiver! yet thou dost wear
The Godhead's most benignant grace;
Nor know we anything so fair
As is the smile upon thy face:
Flowers laugh before thee on their beds
And fragrance in thy footing treads;
Thou dost preserve the stars from wrong;
And the most ancient heavens, through Thee, are
fresh and strong.

To humbler functions, awful Power!
I call thee: I myself commend
Unto thy guidance from this hour;
Oh, let my weakness have an end!
Give unto me, made lowly wise,
The spirit of self-sacrifice;
The confidence of reason give;
And in the light of truth thy Bondman let me live!

# *To -*

## UPON THE BIRTH OF HER FIRST-BORN CHILD, MARCH, 1833

LIKE A shipwrecked Sailor tost
By rough waves on a perilous coast,
Lies the Babe, in helplessness
And in tenderest nakedness,
Flung by labouring Nature forth
Upon the mercies of the earth.
Can its eyes beseech? – no more
Than the hands are free to implore:
Voice but serves for one brief cry;
Plaint was it? or prophecy
Of sorrow that will surely come?
Omen of man's grievous doom!

But, O Mother! by the close
Duly granted to thy throes;
By the silent thanks, now tending
Incense-like to Heaven, descending
Now to mingle and to move
With the gush of earthly love,
As a debt to that frail Creature,
Instrument of struggling Nature
For the blissful calm, the peace
Known but to this one release –
Can the pitying spirit doubt
That for human-kind springs out
From the penalty a sense
Of more than mortal recompense?

As a floating summer cloud,
Though of gorgeous drapery proud,
To the sun-burnt traveller,
Or the stooping labourer,
Oft-times makes its bounty known
By its shadow round him thrown;
So, by chequerings of sad cheer,
Heavenly Guardians, brooding near,
Of their presence tell – too bright
Haply for corporeal sight!
Ministers of grace divine
Feelingly their brows incline
O'er this seeming Castaway
Breathing, in the light of day,
Something like the faintest breath
That has power to baffle death –
Beautiful, while very weakness
Captivates like passive meekness.

And, sweet Mother! under warrant
Of the universal Parent,
Who repays in season due
Them who have, like thee, been true
To the filial chain let down
From his everlasting throne,
Angels hovering round thy couch,
With their softest whispers vouch,
That – whatever griefs may fret,
Cares entangle, sins beset,
This thy First-born, and with tears
Stain her cheek in future years –
Heavenly succour, not denied
To the babe, whate'er betide,
Will to the woman be supplied!

Mother! blest be thy calm ease;
Blest the starry promises, –
And the firmament benign
Hallowed be it, where they shine!
Yes, for them whose souls have scope
Ample for a winged hope,
And can earthward bend an ear
For needful listening, pledge is here,
That, if thy new-born Charge shall tread
In thy footsteps, and be led
By that other Guide, whose light
Of manly virtues, mildly bright,
Gave him first the wished-for part
In thy gentle virgin heart;
Then, amid the storms of life
Presignified by that dread strife
Whence ye have escaped together,
She may look for serene weather;
In all trials sure to find
Comfort for a faithful mind;
Kindlier issues, holier rest,
Than even now await her prest,
Conscious Nursling, to thy breast!

# The Massy Ways

THE MASSY Ways, carried across these heights
By Roman perseverance, are destroyed,
Or hidden under ground, like sleeping worms.
How venture then to hope that Time will spare
This humble Walk? Yet on the mountain's side
A Poet's hand first shaped it; and the steps
Of that same Bard – repeated to and fro
At morn, at noon, and under moonlight skies
Through the vicissitudes of many a year –
Forbade the weeds to creep o'er its grey line.
No longer, scattering to the heedless winds
The vocal raptures of fresh poesy,
Shall he frequent these precincts; locked no more
In earnest converse with beloved Friends,
Here will he gather stores of ready bliss,
As from the beds and borders of a garden
Choice flowers are gathered! But, if Power may spring
Out of a farewell yearning – favoured more
Than kindred wishes mated suitably
With vain regrets – the Exile would consign
This Walk, his loved possession, to the care
Of those pure Minds that reverence the Muse.

# Suggested by the View of Lancaster Castle
## (ON THE ROAD FROM THE SOUTH)

THIS SPOT – at once unfolding sight so fair
Of sea and land, with yon grey towers that still
    Rise up as if to lord it over air –
Might soothe in human breasts the sense of ill,
    Or charm it out of memory; yea, might fill
    The heart with joy and gratitude to God
    For all his bounties upon man bestowed:
Why bears it then the name of 'Weeping Hill'?
Thousands, as toward yon old Lancastrian Towers,
    A prison's crown, along this way they past
For lingering durance or quick death with shame,
    From this bare eminence thereon have cast
Their first look – blinded as tears fell in showers
Shed on their chains; and hence that doleful name.

# Ode

## COMPOSED ON MAY MORNING

WHILE FROM the purpling east departs
The star that led the dawn,
Blithe Flora from her couch upstarts,
For May is on the lawn.
A quickening hope, a freshening glee,
Foreran the expected Power,
Whose first-drawn breath from bush and tree
Shakes off that pearly shower.

All Nature welcomes Her whose sway
Tempers the year's extremes;
Who scattereth lustres o'er noon-day,
Like morning's dewy gleams;
While mellow warble, sprightly trill.
The tremulous heart excite;
And hums the balmy air to still
The balance of delight.

Time was, blest Power! when youths and maids
At peep of dawn would rise,
And wander forth, in forest glades
Thy birth to solemnize.
Though mute the song – to grace the rite
Untouched the hawthorn bough,
Thy Spirit triumphs o'er the slight;
Man changes, but not Thou!

Thy feathered Lieges bill and wings
In love's disport employ;
Warmed by thy influence, creeping things
Awake to silent joy:
Queen art thou still for each gay plant
Where the slim wild deer roves;
And served in depths where fishes haunt
Their own mysterious groves.

Cloud-piercing peak, and trackless heath,
Instinctive homage pay;
Nor wants the dim-lit cave a wreath
To honour thee, sweet May!
Where cities fanned by thy brisk airs
Behold a smokeless sky,
Their puniest flower-pot-nursling dares
To open a bright eye.

And if, on this thy natal morn,
The pole, from which thy name
Hath not departed, stands forlorn
Of song and dance and game;
Still from the village-green a vow
Aspires to thee addrest,
Wherever peace is on the brow,
Or love within the breast.

Yes! where Love nestles thou canst teach
The soul to love the more;
Hearts also shall thy lessons reach
That never loved before.
Stript is the haughty one of pride,
The bashful freed from fear,
While rising, like the ocean-tide,
In flows the joyous year.

Hush, feeble lyre! weak words refuse
The service to prolong!
To yon exulting thrush the Muse
Entrusts the imperfect song;
His voice shall chant, in accents clear,
Throughout the live-long day,
Till the first silver star appear,
The sovereignty of May.

# Weep Not Beloved Friends

WEEP NOT, beloved Friends! nor let the air
For me with sighs be troubled. Not from life
Have I been taken; this is genuine life
And this alone – the life which now I live
In peace eternal; where desire and joy
Together move in fellowship without end. –
Francesco Ceni willed that, after death,
His tombstone thus should speak for him. And surely
Small cause there is for that fond wish of ours
Long to continue in this world; a world
That keeps not faith, nor yet can point a hope
To good, whereof itself is destitute.

# *Lines Composed at Grasmere*
### DURING A WALK ONE EVENING, AFTER A STORMY DAY, THE AUTHOR HAVING JUST READ IN A NEWSPAPER THAT THE DISSOLUTION OF MR FOX WAS HOURLY EXPECTED.

LOUD IS the Vale! the Voice is up
With which she speaks when storms are gone,
A mighty unison of streams!
Of all her Voices, One!

Loud is the Vale; – this inland Depth
In peace is roaring like the Sea;
Yon star upon the mountain-top
Is listening quietly.

Sad was I, even to pain deprest,
Importunate and heavy load!

The Comforter hath found me here,
Upon this lonely road;

And many thousands now are sad –
Wait the fulfilment of their fear;
For he must die who is their stay,
Their glory disappear.

A Power is passing from the earth
To breathless Nature's dark abyss;
But when the great and good depart
What is it more than this –

That Man, who is from God sent forth,
Doth yet again to God return? –
Such ebb and flow must ever be,
Then wherefore should we mourn?

# Composed upon Westminster Bridge September 3, 1802

EARTH HAS not anything to show more fair:
Dull would he be of soul who could pass by
A sight so touching in its majesty:
This City now doth, like a garment, wear
The beauty of the morning; silent, bare,
Ships, towers, domes, theatres, and temples lie
Open unto the fields, and to the sky;
All bright and glittering in the smokeless air.
Never did sun more beautifully steep
In his first splendour, valley, rock, or hill;
Ne'er saw I, never felt, a calm so deep!
The river glideth at his own sweet will:
Dear God! the very houses seem asleep;
And all that mighty heart is lying still!

# To Sleep

A FLOCK of sheep that leisurely pass by,
One after one; the sound of rain, and bees
Murmuring; the fall of rivers, winds and seas,
Smooth fields, white sheets of water, and pure sky;
I have thought of all by turns, and yet do lie
Sleepless! and soon the small birds' melodies
Must hear, first uttered from my orchard trees;
And the first cuckoo's melancholy cry.
Even thus last night, and two nights more, I lay,
And could not win thee, Sleep! by any stealth:
So do not let me wear to-night away:
Without Thee what is all the morning's wealth?
Come, blessed barrier between day and day,
Dear mother of fresh thoughts and joyous health!

# My Heart Leaps Up

MY heart leaps up when I behold
A rainbow in the sky:
So was it when my life began;
So is it now I am a man;
So be it when I shall grow old,
Or let me die!
The Child is father of the Man;
And I could wish my days to be
Bound each to each by natural piety.

# Surprised by Joy

SURPRISED by joy – impatient as the Wind
I turned to share the transport – Oh! with whom
But Thee, deep buried in the silent tomb,
That spot which no vicissitude can find?
Love, faithful love, recalled thee to my mind –
But how could I forget thee? – Through what power,
Even for the least division of an hour,
Have I been so beguiled as to be blind
To my most grievous loss! – That thought's return
Was the worst pang that sorrow ever bore,
Save one, one only, when I stood forlorn,
Knowing my heart's best treasure was no more;
That neither present time, nor years unborn
Could to my sight that heavenly face restore.

# It is a Beauteous Evening

IT IS a beauteous evening, calm and free,
The holy time is quiet as a Nun
Breathless with adoration; the broad sun
Is sinking down in its tranquillity;
The gentleness of heaven broods o'er the Sea:
Listen! the mighty Being is awake,
And doth with his eternal motion make
A sound like thunder – everlastingly.
Dear Child! dear Girl! that walkest with me here,
If thou appear untouched by solemn thought,
Thy nature is not therefore less divine:
Thou liest in Abraham's bosom all the year;
And worshipp'st at the Temple's inner shrine,
God being with thee when we know it not.

# Tintern Abbey

### LINES COMPOSED A FEW MILES ABOVE TINTERN ABBEY, ON REVISITING THE BANKS OF THE WYE DURING A TOUR. JULY 13, 1798

FIVE YEARS have past; five summers, with the length
Of five long winters! and again I hear
These waters, rolling from their mountain-springs
With a sweet inland murmur. – Once again
Do I behold these steep and lofty cliffs,
That on a wild secluded scene impress
Thoughts of more deep seclusion; and connect
The landscape with the quiet of the sky.
The day is come when I again repose
Here, under this dark sycamore, and view
These plots of cottage-ground, these orchard-tufts,
Which at this season, with their unripe fruits,
Are clad in one green hue, and lose themselves
'Mid groves and copses. Once again I see
These hedge-rows, hardly hedge-rows, little lines
Of sportive wood run wild: these pastoral farms,
Green to the very door; and wreaths of smoke
Sent up, in silence, from among the trees!
With some uncertain notice, as might seem
Of vagrant dwellers in the houseless woods,
Or of some hermit's cave, where by his fire
The Hermit sits alone.

These beauteous forms,
Through a long absence, have not been to me
As is a landscape to a blind man's eye:
But oft, in lonely rooms, and 'mid the din
Of towns and cities, I have owed to them,
In hours of weariness, sensations sweet,

Felt in the blood, and felt along the heart;
And passing even into my purer mind,
With tranquil restoration: – feelings too
Of unremembered pleasure: such, perhaps,
As have no slight or trivial influence
On that best portion of a good man's life,
His little, nameless, unremembered, acts
Of kindness and of love. Nor less, I trust,
To them I may have owed another gift,
Of aspect more sublime; that blessed mood,
In which the burthen of the mystery,
In which the heavy and the weary weight
Of all this unintelligible world,
Is lightened: – that serene and blessed mood,
In which the affections gently lead us on, –
Until, the breath of this corporeal frame
And even the motion of our human blood
Almost suspended, we are laid asleep
In body, and become a living soul:
While with an eye made quiet by the power
Of harmony, and the deep power of joy,
We see into the life of things.

If this
Be but a vain belief, yet, oh! how oft –
In darkness and amid the many shapes
Of joyless daylight; when the fretful stir
Unprofitable, and the fever of the world,
Have hung upon the beatings of my heart –
How oft, in spirit, have I turned to thee,
O sylvan Wye! thou wanderer thro' the woods,
How often has my spirit turned to thee!
And now, with gleams of half-extinguished thought,
With many recognitions dim and faint,
And somewhat of a sad perplexity,

The picture of the mind revives again:
While here I stand, not only with the sense
Of present pleasure, but with pleasing thoughts
That in this moment there is life and food
For future years. And so I dare to hope,
Though changed, no doubt, from what I was when first
I came among these hills; when like a roe
I bounded o'er the mountains, by the sides
Of the deep rivers, and the lonely streams,
Wherever nature led: more like a man
Flying from something that he dreads than one
Who sought the thing he loved. For nature then
(The coarser pleasures of my boyish days
And their glad animal movements all gone by)
To me was all in all. – I cannot paint
What then I was. The sounding cataract
Haunted me like a passion: the tall rock,
The mountain, and the deep and gloomy wood,
Their colours and their forms, were then to me
An appetite; a feeling and a love,
That had no need of a remoter charm,
By thought supplied, nor any interest
Unborrowed from the eye. – That time is past,
And all its aching joys are now no more,
And all its dizzy raptures. Not for this
Faint I, nor mourn nor murmur; other gifts
Have followed; for such loss, I would believe,
Abundant recompense. For I have learned
To look on nature, not as in the hour
Of thoughtless youth; but hearing oftentimes
The still, sad music of humanity,
Nor harsh nor grating, though of ample power
To chasten and subdue. And I have felt
A presence that disturbs me with the joy
Of elevated thoughts; a sense sublime

Of something far more deeply interfused,
Whose dwelling is the light of setting suns,
And the round ocean, and the living air,
And the blue sky, and in the mind of man:
A motion and a spirit, that impels
All thinking things, all objects of all thought,
And rolls through all things. Therefore am I still
A lover of the meadows and the woods,
And mountains; and of all that we behold
From this green earth; of all the mighty world
Of eye, and ear, – both what they half create,
And what perceive; well pleased to recognise
In nature and the language of the sense,
The anchor of my purest thoughts, the nurse,
The guide, the guardian of my heart, and soul
Of all my moral being.

Nor perchance,
If I were not thus taught, should I the more
Suffer my genial spirits to decay:
For thou art with me here upon the banks
Of this fair river; thou my dearest Friend,
My dear, dear Friend; and in thy voice I catch
The language of my former heart, and read
My former pleasures in the shooting lights
Of thy wild eyes. Oh! yet a little while
May I behold in thee what I was once,
My dear, dear Sister! and this prayer I make,
Knowing that Nature never did betray
The heart that loved her; 'tis her privilege,
Through all the years of this our life, to lead
From joy to joy: for she can so inform
The mind that is within us, so impress
With quietness and beauty, and so feed
With lofty thoughts, that neither evil tongues

Rash judgements, nor the sneers of selfish men,
Nor greetings where no kindness is, nor all
The dreary intercourse of daily life,
Shall e'er prevail against us, or disturb
Our cheerful faith, that all which we behold
Is full of blessings. Therefore let the moon
Shine on thee in thy solitary walk;
And let the misty mountain-winds be free
To blow against thee: and, in after years,
When these wild ecstasies shall be matured
Into a sober pleasure; when thy mind
Shall be a mansion for all lovely forms,
Thy memory be as a dwelling-place
For all sweet sounds and harmonies; oh! then,
If solitude, or fear, or pain, or grief,
Should be thy portion, with what healing thoughts
Of tender joy wilt thou remember me,
And these my exhortations! Nor, perchance –
If I should be where I no more can hear
Thy voice, nor catch from thy wild eyes these gleams
Of past existence – wilt thou then forget
That on the banks of this delightful stream
We stood together; and that I, so long
A worshipper of Nature, hither came,
Unwearied in that service: rather say
With warmer love – oh! with far deeper zeal
Of holier love. Nor wilt thou then forget,
That after many wanderings, many years
Of absence, these steep woods and lofty cliffs,
And this green pastoral landscape, were to me
More dear, both for themselves and for thy sake!

# The World is Too Much With Us

THE WORLD is too much with us; late and soon,
Getting and spending, we lay waste our powers:
Little we see in Nature that is ours;
We have given our hearts away, a sordid boon!
This Sea that bares her bosom to the moon;
The winds that will be howling at all hours,
And are up-gathered now like sleeping flowers;
For this, for everything, we are out of tune;
It moves us not. – Great God! I'd rather be
A Pagan suckled in a creed outworn;
So might I, standing on this pleasant lea,
Have glimpses that would make me less forlorn;
Have sight of Proteus rising from the sea;
Or hear old Triton blow his wreathed horn.

# *Ode* –

## INTIMATIONS OF IMMORTALITY FROM
## RECOLLECTIONS OF EARLY CHILDHOOD
————— EXTRACT —————

## I

THERE WAS a time when meadow, grove, and stream,
The earth, and every common sight,
To me did seem
Apparelled in celestial light,
The glory and the freshness of a dream.
It is not now as it hath been of yore; –
Turn wheresoe'er I may,
By night or day,
The things which I have seen I now can see no more.

## II

The Rainbow comes and goes,
And lovely is the Rose,
The Moon doth with delight
Look round her when the heavens are bare,
Waters on a starry night
Are beautiful and fair;
The sunshine is a glorious birth;
And yet I know, where'er I go,
That there hath past away a glory from the earth.

# Nuns Fret Not

NUNS FRET not at their convent's narrow room;
And hermits are contented with their cells;
And students with their pensive citadels;
Maids at the wheel, the weaver at his loom,
Sit blithe and happy; bees that soar for bloom,
High as the highest Peak of Furness-fells,
Will murmur by the hour in foxglove bells:
In truth the prison, unto which we doom
Ourselves, no prison is: and hence to me,
In sundry moods, 'twas pastime to be bound
Within the Sonnet's scanty plot of ground;
Pleased if some Souls (for such there needs must be)
Who have felt the weight of too much liberty,
Should find brief solace there, as I have found.

# Hast Thou Seen,
# With Flash Incessant

HAST THOU seen, with flash incessant,
Bubbles gliding under ice,
Bodied forth and evanescent,
No one knows by what device?

Such are thoughts! – A wind-swept meadow
Mimicking a troubled sea,
Such is life; and death a shadow
From the rock eternity!

# Elegiac Stanzas
## —— EXTRACT ——

LULLED BY the sound of pastoral bells,
Rude Nature's Pilgrims did we go,
From the dread summit of the Queen
Of mountains, through a deep ravine,
Where, in her holy chapel, dwells
'Our Lady of the Snow.'

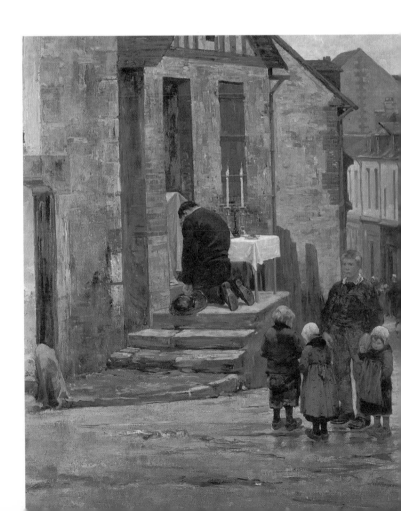

The sky was blue, the air was mild;
Free were the streams and green the bowers;
As if, to rough assaults unknown,
The genial spot has ever shown
A countenance that as sweetly smiled –
The face of summer-hours.

And we were gay, our hearts at ease;
With pleasure dancing through the frame
We journeyed; all we knew of care –
Our path that straggled here and there;
Of trouble – but the fluttering breeze;
Of Winter – but a name.

# An Evening Walk
## —— EXTRACT ——

HUNG O'ER A cloud, above the steep that rears
It's edge all flame, the broad'ning sun appears;
A long blue bar it's ægis orb divides,
And breaks the spreading of it's gold tides;
And now it touches on the purple steep,
That flings his shadow on the pictur'd deep.
Cross the calm lake's blue shades the cliffs aspire,
With tow'rs and woods a 'prospect all on fire;'
The coves and secret hollows thro' a ray
Of fainter gold a purple gleam betray;
The gilded turf arrays in richer green
Each speck of lawn the broken rocks between;
Deep yellow beams the scatter'd boles illume,
Far in the level forest's central gloom;
Waving his hat, the shepherd in the vale
Directs his winding dog the cliffs to scale,
That, barking busy 'mid the glittering rocks,
Hunts, where he points, the intercepted flocks;
Where oaks o'erhang the road the radiance shoots
On tawny earth, wild weeds, and twisted roots;
The Druid stones their lighted fane unfold,
And all the babbling brooks are liquid gold;
Sunk to a curve the day-star lessens still,
Gives one bright glance, and sinks behind the hill.

# The Prelude

—— EXTRACT ——

## BOOK IV – SUMMER VACATION

YES, THAT heartless chase
Of trivial pleasures was a poor exchange
For books and nature at that early age.
'Tis true, some casual knowledge might be gained
Of character or life; but at that time,
Of manners put to school I took small note,
And all my deeper passions lay elsewhere.
Far better had it been to exalt the mind
By solitary study, to uphold
Intense desire through meditative peace;
And yet, for chastisement of these regrets,
The memory of one particular hour
Doth here rise up against me. 'Mid a throng
Of maids and youths, old men, and matrons staid,
A medley of all tempers, I had passed
The night in dancing, gaiety, and mirth,
With din of instruments and shuffling feet,
And glancing forms, and tapers glittering,
And unaimed prattle flying up and down;
Spirits upon the stretch, and here and there
Slight shocks of young love-liking interspersed,
Whose transient pleasure mounted to the head,
And tingled through the veins. Ere we returned,
The cock had crowed, and now the eastern sky
Was kindling, nor unseen, from humble copse
And open field, through which the pathway wound,
And homeward led my steps. Magnificent
The morning rose, in memorable pomp,
Glorious as e'er I had beheld – in front,
The sea lay laughing at a distance; near,

The solid mountains shone, bright as the clouds,
Grain-tinctured, drenched in empyrean light;
And in the meadows and the lower grounds
Was all the sweetness of a common dawn –
Dews, vapours, and the melody of bird,
And labourers going forth to till the fields.
Ah! need I say, dear Friend! that to the brim
My heart was full; I made no vows, but vows
Were then made for me; bond unknown to me
Was given, that I should be, else sinning greatly,
A dedicated Spirit. On I walked
In thankful blessedness, which yet survives.

# Scorn Not the Sonnet

SCORN NOT the Sonnet; Critic, you have frowned,
   Mindless of its just honours; – with this key
   Shakespeare unlocked his heart; the melody
Of this small lute gave ease to Petrarch's wound;
   A thousand times this pipe did Tasso sound;
   With it Camöens soothed an exile's grief;
   The Sonnet glittered a gay myrtle leaf
Amid the cypress with which Dante crowned
   His visionary brow: a glow-worm lamp,
It cheered mild Spenser, called from Faery-land
To struggle through dark ways; and when a damp
   Fell round the path of Milton, in his hand
The Thing became a trumpet; whence he blew
   Soul-animating strains – alas, too few!

# To the Daisy
## —— EXTRACT ——

SWEET FLOWER! belike one day to have
A place upon thy Poet's grave,
I welcome thee once more:
But He, who was on land, at sea,
My Brother, too, in loving thee,
Although he loved more silently,
Sleeps by his native shore.

Ah! hopeful, hopeful was the day
When to that Ship he bent his way,
To govern and to guide:
His wish was gained: a little time
Would bring him back in manhood's prime
And free for life, these hills to climb,
With all his wants supplied.

And full of hope day followed day
While that stout Ship at anchor lay
Beside the shores of Wight;
The May had then made all things green;
And, floating there, in pomp serene,
That Ship was goodly to be seen,
His pride and his delight.

Yet then, when called ashore, he sought
The tender peace of rural thought:
In more than happy mood
To your abodes, bright daisy Flowers!
He then would steal at leisure hours,
And loved you glittering in your bowers
A starry multitude.

# The Excursion
## BOOK I – THE WANDERER
———— EXTRACT ————

HE CEASED. Ere long the sun declining shot
A slant and mellow radiance, which began
To fall upon us, while, beneath the trees,
We sate on that low bench: and now we felt,
Admonished thus, the sweet hour coming on.
A linnet warbled from those lofty elms,
A thrush sang loud, and other melodies,
At distance heard, peopled the milder air.
The old Man rose, and, with a sprightly mien
Of hopeful preparation, grasped his staff;
Together casting then a farewell look
Upon those silent walls, we left the shade;
And, ere the stars were visible, had reached
A village-inn, – our evening resting-place.

# Index to First Lines

# Notes on Illustrations